SRSLY. BEST. JOKES. EVER.

JOKES for KIDS

CHANTELLE GRACE

BroadStreet
PUBLISHING

BroadStreet Kids
Racine, Wisconsin, USA

BroadStreet Kids is an imprint of BroadStreet Publishing Group, LLC.
Broadstreetpublishing.com

SRSLY.BEST.JOKES.EVER.

ISBN 978-1-4245- 5465-2
Content compiled by Chantelle Grace.

Design by Chris Garborg | garborgdesign.com
Editorial services by Michelle Winger | literallyprecise.com

Printed in the United States of America.

17   18   19   20   21   22   23   7   6   5   4   3   2   1

Author Bio

CHANTELLE GRACE is a witty wordsmith who loves music, art, and competitive games. She is fascinated by God's intricate design of the human body. As she works her way through medical school, she knows it's important to share the gift of laughter with those around her. When she's not studying abroad, she makes her home in Prior Lake, Minnesota.

TABLE OF CONTENTS .....

COLOR COMEDY

What happens when you throw a white hat into the Black Sea?

It gets wet.

What's black and white, black and white, and black and white?

A zebra caught in a revolving door.

What's black and white, black and white, and green?

Two skunks fighting over a pickle.

When is a black dog not a black dog?

When it's a grey-hound.

Why did the tomato turn red?

Because it saw the salad dressing.

What's orange and sounds like a parrot?

A carrot.

What bird is always sad?

The blue jay.

What's green and smells like blue paint?

Green paint.

What color is a burp?

Burple.

What do you do when you find
a blue elephant?

Cheer it up.

What do you do with a green monster?

Wait until it's ripe.

What happened when a red ship crashed
into a blue ship?

The crew was marooned.

What would you call the USA if everyone
had a pink car?

A pink carnation.

What is a cheerleader's favorite color?

Yeller.

GEOGRAPHY GIGGLES

What goes through towns, up and over hills, but doesn't move?

The road.

What did the little mountain say to the big mountain?

"Hi Cliff."

What do you call a funny mountain?

Hill-arious.

What is the best day to go
to the beach?

Sunday, of course.

What stays on the ground
but never gets dirty?

A shadow.

Name a city where no one goes?

Electricity.

What stays in the corner and travels
all over the world?

A stamp.

What is the tallest building
in the world?

*The library because it has
the most stories.*

What did the stamp say
to the envelope?

"Stick with me and we will go places."

What did the ground say
to the earthquake?

"You crack me up."

Why does the Mississippi river
see so well?

Because it has 4 i's.

MONEY MADNESS

Where does a penguin keep its money?

In a snow bank.

Where do fish keep their money?

In a river-bank.

How do dinosaurs pay their bills?

With Tyrannosaurus checks.

Where can you always find money?

In the dictionary.

Why did the robber take a bath
before he stole from the bank?

He wanted to make a clean getaway.

What did one penny say
to the other penny?

"Together we make cents."

What is brown and has a head
and a tail but no legs?

A penny.

What did the duck say after
he went shopping?

"Put it on my bill."

What did the football coach say
to the broken vending machine?

"Give me my quarterback."

What has a hundred heads
and a hundred tails?

One hundred pennies.

Why can't you borrow money
from a leprechaun?

Because they're always a little short.

Why didn't the quarter roll down the hill
with the nickel?

Because it had more cents.

What English word has three
consecutive double letters?

Bookkeeper.

Where does success
come before work?

In the dictionary.

Why did the businessman put a clock
under his desk?

*Because he wanted
to work over-time.*

SCHOOL SILLIES

Why did the nose not want to go to school?

It was tired of getting picked on.

How do you get straight A's?

By using a ruler.

What did the pen say to the pencil?

"So, what's your point?"

Why did the kid study in the airplane?

*Because he wanted
a higher education.*

How did the music teacher get locked
out of the classroom?

His keys were inside the piano.

What do elves learn in school?

The elf-abet.

What did you learn in school today?

*Not enough,
I have to go back tomorrow.*

What object is king of the classroom?

The ruler.

What did the pencil sharpener say to the pencil?

"Stop going in circles and get to the point."

What do librarians take with them when they go fishing?

Bookworms.

What vegetables do librarians like?

Peas.

Why did the clock in the cafeteria run slow?

It always went back four seconds.

Why didn't the sun go to college?

Because it already had a million degrees.

Where do the pianists go for vacation?

The Florida Keys.

What is the smartest state?

Alabama—it has four A's and one B.

What did the paper say to the pencil?

"Write on."

What kind of meals do math teachers eat?

Square meals.

Teacher: Now class, whatever I ask, I want you to all answer at once. How much is six plus four?

Class: At once.

Why didn't the two 4's want
any dinner?

   Because they already 8.

What is a math teacher's
favorite season?

   Sum-mer.

What is a butterfly's favorite subject
at school?

   Mothematics.

What do you get when you divide
the circumference of a Jack-o-lantern
by its diameter?

   Pumpkin Pi.

What did zero say to the number eight?

   "Nice belt."

Teacher: Why are you doing your multiplication on the floor?

Student: You told me not to use tables.

Why did the teacher wear sunglasses?

Because his class was so bright.

Teacher: Didn't I tell you to stand at the end of the line?

Student: I tried but there was someone already there.

How is an English teacher like a judge?

They both give out sentences.

Teacher: You missed school yesterday, didn't you?

Student: Not really.

Why did the teacher go to the beach?

To test the water.

Teacher: If I had six oranges in one hand
and seven apples in the other,
what would I have?

Student: Big hands.

Teacher: If you got $20 from five
people, what would you have?

Student: A new bike.

Teacher: I hope I didn't see you looking
at John's exam.

Student: I hope you didn't either.

Teacher: What is the shortest month?

*Student: May—it only has
three letters.*

Why did the teacher turn the lights on?

Because his class was so dim.

What do you do if a teacher rolls
her eyes at you?

Pick them up and roll them back.

Why did the teacher write
on the window?

*Because he wanted the lesson
to be very clear.*

Why was everyone so tired on April 1st?

*They had just finished
a March of 31 days.*

Which hand is it better to write with?

Neither, it's best to write with a pen.

Why does the calendar seem
so popular?

It has so many dates.

Why did the music teacher need
a ladder?

To reach the high notes.

What's the worst thing you're likely
to find in the school cafeteria?

The food.

Why aren't you doing well in history?

*Because the teacher keeps asking
about things that happened before
I was born.*

What has forty feet and sings?

The school choir.

What makes music on your head?

A head band.

In which school do you learn
to make ice cream?

Sundae school.

CLOTHING CHEER

What do you call a belt
with a watch on it?

A waist of time.

What did the tie say to the hat?

*"You go on ahead
and I'll hang around."*

Why did the woman go outdoors
with her purse open?

*Because she expected some change
in the weather.*

Why don't you wear a cardboard belt?

That would be a waist of paper.

Why did the clown wear loud socks?

So his feet wouldn't fall asleep.

Why did the leopard wear
a striped shirt?

So it wouldn't be spotted.

What's the biggest problem
with snow boots?

They melt.

What do you call doing 2,000 pounds
of laundry?

Washing-ton.

What kind of shoes do all spies wear?

Sneakers.

Does your shirt have holes in it?

No.

Then how did you put it on?

SPORTS SLAPSTICK

Why can't Cinderella play soccer?

Because she's always running away from the ball.

When is a baby good at basketball?

When it's dribbling.

Why do basketball players love donuts?

Because they dunk them.

What's a golfer's favorite letter?

T.

What do you call a pig
who plays basketball?

A ball hog.

Why did the golfer wear two pairs
of pants?

In case he got a hole in one.

How is a baseball team similar
to a pancake?

They both need a good batter.

What animal is best at hitting
a baseball?

A bat.

At what sport do waiters do really well?

Tennis, because they can serve.

How do football players stay cool
during the game?

They stand close to the fans.

What is an insect's favorite sport?

Cricket.

What do hockey players and magicians
have in common?

Both do hat tricks.

Why did the man keep doing
the backstroke?

*Because he just ate and didn't want
to swim on a full stomach.*

What is the hardest part
about skydiving?

The ground.

KNOCK-KNOCK KNEE-SLAPPERS

Knock, knock.

Who's there?

Little old lady.

Little old lady who?

Wow! I didn't know you could yodel.

Knock, knock.

Who's there?

Cowsgo.

2.

Cowsgo who?

No they don't; cowsgo moo.

Knock, knock.

Who's there?

3.

Interrupting cow.

Interrupting cow wh...

Moo!

Knock, knock.

Who's there?

Doris.

Doris who?

Doris locked; that's why I knocked.

Knock, knock.

Who's there?

Cash.

Cash who?

I knew you were a nut.

Knock, knock.

Who's there?

Ash.

Ash who?

Bless you.

Knock, knock.

Who's there?

Nobel.

Nobel who?

No bell, that's why I knocked.

Knock, knock.

Who's there?

Leaf.

Leaf who?

Leaf me alone.

Knock, knock.

Who's there?

Lettuce.

Lettuce who?

Lettuce in and you'll find out.

Knock, knock.

Who's there?

Aaron.

Aaron who?

Why Aaron you opening the door?

Knock, knock.

Who's there?

Tank.

Tank who?

You're welcome.

Knock, knock.

Who's there?

Hawaii.

Hawaii who?

I'm fine; Hawaii you?

Knock, knock.

Who's there?

Orange.

Orange who?

Orange you even going to open the door?

Knock, knock.

Who's there?

Who.

Who who?

Is there an owl in there?

Knock, knock.

Who's there?

Anita.

Anita who?

Anita borrow a pencil.

Knock, knock.

Who's there?

Figs.

Figs who?

Figs the doorbell; it's broken.

Knock, knock.

Who's there?

Alice.

Alice who?

Alice fair in love and war.

Knock, knock.

Who's there?

Annie.

Annie who?

*Annie thing you can do
I can do better.*

Knock, knock.

Who's there?

Yukon.

Yukon who?

Yukon say that again.

Knock, knock.

Who's there?

Boo.

Boo who?

Well you don't have to cry about it.

Knock, knock.

Who's there?

Theodore.

Theodore who?

Theodore is stuck and it won't open.

Knock, knock.

Who's there?

Cher.

Cher who?

Cher would be nice if you opened the door.

Knock, knock

Who's there?

Amos.

Amos who?

A mosquito bit me.

Knock, knock.

Who's there?

Police.

Police who?

Police let us in; it's cold out here.

Knock, knock.

Who's there?

Amarillo.

Amarillo who?

Amarillo nice guy.

Knock, knock.

Who's there?

Irish.

Irish who?

Irish you a happy St. Patrick's Day.

Knock, knock.

Who's there?

Kook.

Kook who?

Don't call me cuckoo!

NATURE NONSENSE

How can you tell that a tree
is a dogwood tree?

By its bark.

What kind of hair do oceans have?

Wavy.

What kind of flower grows on your
face?

Tulips.

What did the little tree say
to the big tree?

"Leaf me alone."

Why did the girl bring a book
and a pen to the garden?

She wanted to weed and write.

Did you hear the one about
the oak tree?

It's a-corny one.

Where does seaweed go to look
for a job?

The kelp wanted section.

What did the big flower say
to the little flower?

"Hey, bud."

Why did the pine tree get into trouble?

Because it was being knotty.

How can you tell the ocean is friendly?

It waves.

What did the tree do when
the bank closed?

It started a new branch.

Who cleans the bottom of the ocean?

A mer-maid.

What washes up on very small beaches?

Microwaves.

What flower doesn't tell the truth?

A li-lac.

What did the gardener say when she dropped her flowers?

"Whoopsie daises."

FARM FUNNIES

What's a cow's favorite game?

Moosical chairs.

What do you call a pig with no legs?

A groundhog.

What kind of car does a farmer drive?

A cornvertable.

How do pigs write top secret messages?

With invisible oink.

How did the farmer mend his pants?

With cabbage patches.

What do you call a sheep with no head and no legs?

A cloud.

Where do cows go for entertainment?

To the moo-vies.

Why did the farmer ride his horse to town?

It was too heavy to carry.

Where do sheep go on vacation?

To the baaaaaahamas.

What do you call a happy cowboy?

A jolly rancher. What

What is a pig's favorite color?

Mahogany.

How do you fit more pigs on your farm?

Build a sty-scraper.

When does a horse talk?

Whinny wants to.

What did the farmer call the cow
that had no milk?

An udder failure.

What do you call a sheep covered in chocolate?

A candy baa.

What do you call an emotional cow?

Moo-dy.

What do you get when you play Tug-of-War with a pig?

Pulled pork.

What does a mixed-up hen lay?

Scrambled eggs.

Why did the pig cross the road?

He got boared.

What sickness do horses hate the most?

Hay fever!

How do you take a sick pig to the hospital?

In a hambulance.

What's the most musical part of a chicken?

The drumstick.

What do you call a pig that drives recklessly?

A road hog.

What is a sheep's favorite game?

Baa-dminton.

Where do you find a chicken
with no legs?

Exactly where you left it.

What's the difference between
a horse and the weather?

*One is reined up and the other
rains down.*

What do you get when you cross
a cow and a duck?

Milk and quackers.

Where do bulls get their messages?

On a bull-etin board.

What do you call a cow that won't
give milk?

A milk dud.

Who is the smartest pig in the world?

Ein-swine.

What do you call it when it rains
chickens and ducks?

Foul weather.

What did the bad sheep want to do?

Wool the world.

Have you heard about
the cow astronaut?

He landed on the moooon.

Where do sheep go
to get their haircut?

The baabaa shop.

Why did the cow cross the road?

To get to the udder side.

Why do cows wear bells?

Their horns don't work.

What do you get when you cross a cow and a goat?

A coat.

What do you call a cow that plays a musical instrument?

A moo-sician.

What does it mean if you find a horseshoe in the road?

Some poor horse is walking around in its socks.

What do you call a sleeping bull?

A bull dozer.

Why did the turkey cross the road?

It was the chicken's day off.

Which side of a chicken
has the most feathers?

The outside.

Why do hens lay eggs?

If they dropped them, they'd break.

What do you get if you cross a chicken
with a cow?

Roost beef.

What do you call a horse that lives next door?

A neigh-bor.

Why did the cow jump over the moon?

Because the farmer had cold hands!

SPACE
SIDE-SPLITTERS

Why didn't people like the restaurant on the moon?

Because there was no atmosphere.

What do astronauts cook on?

Flying saucers.

Why did the baby go to outer space?

To visit the milky way.

What does an astronaut use to keep
his feet warm?

A space heater.

How do you know when the moon
is going broke?

When it's down to its last quarter.

How does the barber cut
the moon's hair?

E-clipse it.

What holds the sun up in the sky?

Sunbeams.

What is the center of gravity?

The letter V.

What do you call a peanut
in a spacesuit?

An astronut.

What did the alien say to the garden?

Take me to your weeder.

What kind of plates do they use
on Venus?

Flying saucers.

What does an astronaut eat
for dinner?

Nothing, he went out for launch.

TRANSPORTATION THRILLS

When does a cart come before a horse?

In the dictionary.

Why don't traffic lights ever go swimming?

Because they take too long to change.

What vehicle did the crazy man drive?

A loco-motive.

Why did the man put his car
in the oven?

He wanted a hot rod.

What is a motorcycle called
when it laughs?

A Yamahahaha.

What does a houseboat turn into
when it grows up?

A township.

What only starts to work after
it's fired?

A rocket.

What's the worst vegetable to serve
on a boat?

Leeks.

How do trains hear?

Through their engine-ears.

What did one elevator say to the other elevator?

"I think I'm coming down with something."

What do you call a flying police officer?

A helicopper.

What kind of car did the Pilgrims drive?

A Plymouth.

RIDDLE RIOTS

David's father had three sons:
Snap, Crackle, and...?

David.

If you were in a race and passed
the person in second place,
what place would you be in?

Second place.

What word looks the same backwards
and upside down?

Swims.

What gets bigger and bigger as you take more away from it?

A hole.

How many months have 28 days?

All of them.

What has two hands, a round face, always runs, but stays in place?

A clock.

What breaks when you say it?

Silence.

Can you spell rotten with two letters?

DK.

How can you spell cold with two letters?

IC.

What starts with a P, ends with an E, and has a hundred letters in it?

Post Office.

What can run but can't walk?

The water faucet.

What is taken before you get it?

Your picture.

A rooster laid an egg on a barn roof. Which way would it roll?

Roosters don't lay eggs, hens do.

Chickens rise when the rooster crows,
but when do ducks get up?

At the quack of dawn.

Why can't your nose be 12 inches long?

Because then it would be a foot.

Why did the lazy man want a job
in a bakery?

So he could loaf around.

What goes up, but never comes down?

Your age.

What is full of holes but can still
hold water?

A sponge.

What's as big as a dinosaur
but weighs nothing?

Its shadow.

What cheese is made backwards?

Edam.

What geometric figure is like
a lost parrot?

A polygon.

Why do dogs run in circles?

*Because it's too hard to run
in squares.*

How do you confuse a fish?

*Put it in a round fishbowl
and tell it to go to the corner.*

What do you call a line of rabbits
walking backwards?

A receding hareline.

What does a thesaurus eat
for breakfast?

A synonym roll.

What do you get when you cross an owl
and an oyster?

Pearls of wisdom.

What letter can hurt you if you get
too close?

B.

What do you call fifty penguins
at the North Pole?

*Really lost, because penguins live
in the Southern Hemisphere.*

What's worse than a worm
in your apple?

Half a worm in your apple.

Why are A's like flowers?

Because bees come after them.

What do you call a fly without wings?

A walk.

HOLIDAY HILARITY

Why did pilgrims' pants always fall down?

Because they wore their belt buckle on their hat.

Why does Santa Claus like to go down the chimney?

Because it soots him!

What happened when the Thanksgiving turkey got into a fight?

He got the stuffing knocked out of him.

What do Santa's elves do after school?

Their gnomework!

Why do students do so poorly
after Thanksgiving?

*Because everything gets marked
down after the holidays.*

Why didn't the skeleton go
to the dance?

Because he had no-body to go with.

What always comes at the end
of Thanksgiving?

The G.

What do snowmen like to eat
for breakfast?

Frosted Flakes.

Who isn't hungry on Thanksgiving?

The turkey, because he's already stuffed.

Why don't skeletons fight?

They don't have the guts.

What happens when a snowman throws a temper tantrum?

He has a meltdown.

DINOSAUR DRAMA

What do you call a dinosaur that smashes everything in its path?

Tyrannosaurus wrecks.

Why did the dinosaur paint her toenails red?

So she could hide in the strawberry patch.

What do you call a tyrannosaurus that talks and talks and talks?

A dino-bore.

What should you do if you find
a dinosaur in your bed?

Find somewhere else to sleep.

What do you get when a dinosaur walks
through the strawberry patch?

Strawberry jam.

How did the dinosaur feel after
he ate a pillow?

Down in the mouth.

What do you get when a dinosaur
sneezes?

Out of the way.

What do you get if you cross
a Triceratops with a kangaroo?

A Tricera-hops.

What do you get if you cross a pig
with a dinosaur?

Jurassic Pork.

Which dinosaurs were
the best policemen?

Tricera-cops.

Where do prehistoric reptiles like
to go on vacation?

To the dino-shore.

How do dinosaurs pay their bills?

With Tyrannosaurus checks.

Why did the Apatosaurus devour
the factory?

Because she was a plant eater.

How can you tell if there's a dinosaur in the refrigerator?

The door won't close.

How do you make a dinosaur float?

Put a scoop of ice cream in a glass of root beer and add a dinosaur.

FOOD FRENZY

How do you make a milk shake?

Give it a good scare.

How do you make a walnut laugh?

Crack it up.

Why did the girl sprinkle sugar on her pillow before she went to sleep?

So she would have sweet dreams.

What kind of keys do kids like to carry?

Cookies!

Why don't they serve chocolate in prison?

Because it makes you break out.

What is a scarecrow's favorite fruit?

Straw-berries.

What does a nosey pepper do?

It gets jalapeno business.

What do you call a fake noodle?

An impasta.

What do you call cheese that doesn't belong to you?

Nacho cheese!

Why did the boy go out with a prune?

Because he couldn't find a date.

Have you heard the joke about
the butter?

I better not tell you; it might spread.

What runs but doesn't get anywhere?

A refrigerator.

What kind of crackers do firemen
like the most?

Firecrackers.

Why was the cookie sad?

*Because its mom was a wafer
too long.*

Why did the boy stare at the label
on the orange juice all day?

Because the carton said concentrate.

ANIMAL ANTICS

How do rabbits stay in shape?

They do a lot of hare-obics.

What do you call a pile of kittens?

A meowntain.

What kind of bird can carry
the most weight?

The crane.

What animal gets in trouble at school?

The cheetah.

Is it raining cats and dogs?

It's okay, as long as it doesn't rein-deer.

Did you hear the story about the peacock?

Yes, it's a beautiful tale.

What bird is with you at every meal?

A swallow.

How do you catch a squirrel?

Climb up a tree and act like a nut.

Why don't you see penguins in the United Kingdom?

Because they're afraid of Wales.

What do you get if you cross a chili pepper, a shovel, and a terrier?

A hot-diggity-dog.

What do you give a sick bird?

Tweetment.

What is a frog's favorite cold drink?

Croak-a-cola.

What do you call a rabbit comedian?

A funny bunny.

What do you call a lizard who is elected to Congress?

Rep. Tile.

Did you hear about the dog who had puppies on the side of the road?

It got a ticket for littering.

Why can't a leopard hide?

It will always be spotted.

What is it called when a cat wins a dog show?

A cat-has-trophy.

What does a duck like to eat with soup?

Quackers.

What did the dog say when he sat on sandpaper?

"Ruff."

Why do birds fly south for the winter?

Because it's too far to walk.

How does a penguin build its house?

Igloos it together.

How can you tell which are
the oldest rabbits?

Just look for the gray hares.

Who did Bambi invite to his
birthday party?

His nearest and deer-est friends.

Why do hummingbirds hum?

Because they forgot the words.

What do frogs wear on their feet?

Open toad shoes.

Why don't oysters share their pearls?

Because they're shellfish.

What do you get when you cross
a walrus with a bee?

A wallaby.

Where do fish sleep?

On a seabed.

What's noisier than a whooping crane?

A trumpeting swan.

What do dogs eat at the movies?

Pup-corn.

What kind of book does a rabbit like to read?

One with a hoppy ending.

What do you call a bird in the winter?

Brrr-d.

What is the strongest creature in the sea?

A mussel.

What do you get if you cross a canary and a 50-foot long snake?

A sing-a-long.

What happens when a duck flies
upside down?

It quacks up.

What do you get when you cross
a parrot and a shark?

A bird that talks your ear off.

How do mice feel when they are sick?

Mouserable.

What do you call a duck who leads
an orchestra?

A con-duck-tor.

What do you get when you cross a frog
and a popsicle?

A hopsicle.

Where do fish go when their things go missing?

The Lost-and-Flounder Department.

How do penguins drink?

Out of beak-ers.

What did the Dalmatian say after eating dinner?

"That hit the spot."

What did the duck wear to his wedding?

A Duxedo.

What is a dog's favorite dessert?

Pup-cakes.

What do you get if you cross a dog
and an airplane?

A jet setter.

What do you call a frog
with no hind legs?

Unhoppy.

Which animal grows down?

A duck.

How do oysters call their friends?

On shell phones.

Why didn't the butterfly go
to the dance?

Because it was a moth ball.

What do you call a wet baby owl?

A moist-owlette.

What's the difference between a guitar
and a fish?

You can't tuna fish.

Where do chimps get their information?

From the ape vine.

What do you call a bear caught
in the rain?

A drizzly bear.

When did the fly fly?

When the spider spied her.

What did the buffalo say to his son
when he left for college?

Bison.

Why did the cowboy buy a daschund?

*Someone told him to get along little
doggy.*

What do penguins wear on their heads?

Ice caps.

What do you get when you cross a frog
and a bunny?

A ribbit.

Why did the owl invite his friends over?

He didn't want to be owl by himself.

What did one frog say to the other?

"Time is fun when you're having flies."

What is a frog's favorite music?

Hip hop.

What do you get when you cross
a penguin and an alligator?

*I don't know, but don't try to fix
its bow tie.*

What do you call two ants that run
away to get married?

Ant-elopes.

How do fleas travel from place to place?

They itch-hike.

What do you get if you cross a centipede and a parrot?

A walkie-talkie.

What are caterpillars afraid of?

Dogger-pillars.

What is an insect's favorite sport?

Cricket.

What kind of fly has a frog in its throat?

A hoarse fly.